The Eating Knife

poems

Ayelet Amittay

Fernwood
PRESS

The Eating Knife

©2025 by Ayelet Amittay

Fernwood Press
Newberg, Oregon
www.fernwoodpress.com

Printed in the United States of America

Cover and page design: Mareesa Fawver Moss
Cover art: "Pa' Que Me Quieras Por Siempre"
    (To Make Me Love You Forever, 1991)
    by Belkis Ayón, used with permission
Author photo: Shimizu Photograph (Eugene, Oregon)

ISBN 978-1-59498-154-8

The contents of this book do not constitute
medical or mental health treatment
or indicate a treatment relationship.

Backlit by two overarching themes—the Binding of Isaac and the mental illness that overtakes the poet's father—*The Eating Knife* skillfully conflates the biblical and the contemporary. Amittay's lyrical speaker traverses landscapes as disparate as Mount Mariah and state hospital waiting rooms and holds up for inquiry subject matter as diverse as boy-band lyrics, Sharon Olds' poems, and a Talmudic debate on the parameters of the command to honor one's parents. Imbued with imagination, pathos, and sophistication, these vignettes surprise and shimmer. Some of them—such as "Years from Then"—will break your heart.

—YEHOSHUA NOVEMBER
author of *Two Worlds Exist*

"None of us imagined ourselves here,/ but here we are" writes Ayelet Amittay, locating herself on a quaking map of silence and story, sacred text and personal narrative. This collection interrogates the "heritable silence[s]" that come to us through family, history, and tradition. The story of the Binding of Isaac haunts each page, as a prism through which the author examines her own "dark familial." Each sparse and piercing poem reiterates: trauma is never an individual experience. Nor is suffering, beauty, healing, or the human search for what's holy. Instead, we are braided together by ancient archetypes and the after-echoes of violence. This generous collection is a tapestry of forms: ekphrastics and abecedarians, a burning haibun and reversed scriptures. Amittay's poems "strike awake the wick." They will enter you and stay with you, "sleeping inside your body/ at the edge of God."

—MÓNICA GOMERY
author of *Might Kindred*

In her stunning debut collection, Ayelet Amittay probes primal, evergreen questions of sacrifice: what is asked, of whom, by whom, upon what altars. The biblical infant Isaac prostrated on a rock, a father unable to stamp out the voices burning in his head, a daughter as witness to and conduit of the lineages we inherit and inhabit—their codices, chemistries, and undertows. Empathetic and exquisitely crafted, *The Eating Knife* wrestles with complex intimacies, turning language to its sacred work as the means by which we reach toward reckoning, love, and wisdom, and those things reach back.

—LISA OLSTEIN
author of *Dream Apartment* and *Pain Studies*

Sharp, swift, and unsparing—the poems in Ayelet Amittay's debut collection, *The Eating Knife*, are much like the book's titular object. They glint in the light of our attention; they awaken to violence when held in our hands. "Tender/ the tinder bed, snap twigs/ to kindling, strike awake the wick," Amittay writes, describing—in characteristically lush language—an altar built for a child. That'd be Isaac, of course. Abraham's not far behind. Those two figures and the blade that nearly passes between them are central to this collection. Amittay reflects on them, reanimates them, and in doing so, undoes that knife's work. She binds a father to his daughter, a biblical story to that father's true crime. I lost track of the lines that I loved. I reveled in how Amittay sets each poem down as effortlessly as cutlery in a drawer. *The Eating Knife* is an exceptional and unflinching debut.

—DEREK MONG
author of *The Identity Thief*

for my brothers

Contents

תָּנוּ רַבָּנָן אֵיזֶהוּ מוֹרָא וְאֵיזֶהוּ כִּיבּוּד מוֹרָא לֹא עוֹמֵד בִּמְקוֹמוֹ
וְלֹא יוֹשֵׁב בִּמְקוֹמוֹ וְלֹא סוֹתֵר אֶת דְּבָרָיו וְלֹא מַכְרִיעוֹ כִּיבּוּד
מַאֲכִיל וּמַשְׁקֶה מַלְבִּישׁ וּמְכַסֶּה מַכְנִיס וּמוֹצִיא

The Sages taught: What is fear and what is honor? Fear of one's father includes the following: One may not stand in his father's fixed place, and may not sit in his place, and may not contradict his statements by expressing an opinion contrary to that of his father, and he may not choose sides when his father argues with someone else. What is considered honor? He gives his father food and drink, dresses and covers him, and brings him in and takes him out for all his household needs.

—Kiddushin 31b,
The William Davidson Talmud
(ed. Koren-Steinsaltz)

How to Build an Altar

Leave it room

              to breathe. Tender
              the tinder bed, snap twigs
              to kindling, strike awake the wick.

Bracken, bramble, imagine the wood
with a fire in its heart. Animals
flee with their mouths open—

              a son, bound as eggshell
              binds a yolk whole and golden,
              unafraid. A father may slake

his knife, but a son can still live
if he imagines the broken branches
whole again, lets the timbers

              turn back into trees.

Self-Portrait as Isaac

I was a youth—yearling,
black bristling my lip.

When you took the knife, I became
still. Thought and wonder
peeled away like burnt bark,

raw underneath. A pair of eyes
just seeing, and breath, and a pulse—

Inside my death the possible
permanence of you
like time moving backward

into the time when I was
half a genetic halo,
half a heap of petals

sleeping inside your body
at the edge of God.

Reversed

Genesis 22:10 –> 22:1

To slay his son

Abraham picked up the knife

on top of the wood and

on the altar—

Isaac. He laid him,

he bound his son.

He laid out the wood,

an altar there.

Abraham built

which God had told him

at the place

they arrived.

My son and

this burnt offering.

To the sheep, for

it is God who will see

and Abraham said

the burnt offering.

Is the sheep for

wood, but where

the firestone and the

son? And he said, here are

and he answered, yes my

father, Abraham, *father.*

Then Isaac said to his.

I Visit the State Hospital

The metal detector is a long electric
sigh, a door without
the rationale of walls.
It cries at the smallest thing.
So I am told to walk through without shoes,
like wading into a river—

guards with their blunt, gloved
hands pat down my arms and legs
for what they imagine I have hidden:
food, toothbrush? I'm not thinking

about a knife, the reason why
he's here. Soon he'll see me
face to face, seconds
will click into place
like gun parts. I will start
smiling before they walk him in.
When he comes through the door,
I am prepared.

The Voice of God

In the first grade I kneel behind a trash can heaped with crepe-paper flames. The branches shudder. I am God's voice. I am God's call for burnt offerings, the scent of smoking flesh. Mount Moriah unspools its summit road down the middle of the reading rug, Abraham climbs, leading God's burnt offering by the hand. The span between the knife and Isaac's chest is a form of closeness. The ram like an afterthought—enough testing now, let us eat. My father shudders in the small attic room of his sickness. My father stamps on the voices in his head, but they keep burning. Soon he will come downstairs. The angel will not stay his hand.

The Eating Knife (הַמַּאֲכֶלֶת)

Bloodless meat on the cutting board.
I don't like cooking or horror
films. I want to heal the tender
center of the wound just
by thinking it. A knife has no ear,
but cheek. No hand, but handle. No
eye, but spine.
I sharpened
my femur
until one edge would
slice you, left one
edge dull as a horizon.
No foot, but heel. No
chest, but belly.
I won't imagine the muscle
needed
to stab her and then
yourself,
won't ask what song
you let loose
when you cut
yourself open.

Who Made Me in Your Image
(שֶׁעָשַׂנִי בְּצֶלֶם)

My father's brother's name was Abraham
but he broke ranks with fate and didn't return

from Mount Moriah. My father was wood
bound in cords, stacked, to be burnt

in his own brightness. Even the few
who made it out unscathed, by which I mean

alive and mentally intact,
are flushed with father-wrath like too much sun.

By the mechitzah the women stand
(here I am

with them)
watch as the favored

and cursed gender unspools,
man into son into seed.

Element

after Shira Erlichman

Lithium adheres to lipids, binds to my milk, all fat and song. The baby latches on and sucks. Filtered by the kidneys, over time the harm accretes. Over time, the thyroid burns out like a star. The baby has no choice; she will be Lithium's patient too. Or, I could keep her safe, not take Lithium, let the horror lick my ankles, slobber on my wrists. Lithium, I transformed myself into a nurse to run this gauntlet, to warden this prison of a brain. My whole life tilting toward this whirl. Lithium, you and I, we choose who is worth saving.

Sometimes the Voices

Sang in a choir. Sapped his strength. Scalded his hand. Seared his steak. Seeped into the horsehair plaster of the attic. Sent him packing. Shot in the dark. Skipped to my Lou. Smelled smoke. Spared his life. Spiked his drink. Spat and polished. Spoke in tongues. Sprung his coil. Stood for selection on the train platform. Suggested alternate endings. Sweated profusely. Sweetened his tea. Swept his floors. Swore he was hearing the truth.

Stenotype

If speech survives

a courtroom, unstruck

from the record, it's

broken, coded

as abbreviation: 22

keys, a ticker tape of white

margin space, no man's

land where letters stand for

pause, punctuation

S   T   PH   =   question

mark in a topography

of neighbor keys. Your Honor,

may I approach

the bench to stand before the court

reporter, beg an alternate

ending? <Question> Surely

some repair can come to

this interstitial

brokenness:

missing consonants   missing

I and why.

"MMMMBop" was released

in 1997, the year my father
was deported. His beard uncombed
as starlight. His crime couldn't sing
without a tongue. That spring without
him, the Hanson brothers lilting
"MMMBop" sunshine, the flowers
growing or not growing under the bleachers
of the high school, "MMMBop" I walked
home alone in fear of anyone
who'd see the murderer in me.
In the song's parlay "MMMBop"
is pop for the unsayable
but cheerfully, the reverse
of a black hole, or of my father
with his back to me—can you tell me?

Burning Burnt Offering Haibun

Genesis 22:1-21

I

Some time afterward, God put Abraham to the test, saying to
him, "Abraham." He answered, "Here I am." "Take your son,
your favored one, Isaac, whom you love, and go to the land of
Moriah, and offer him there as a burnt offering on one of the
heights that I will point out to you."
So early next morning, Abraham saddled his ass and took with
him two of his servants and his son Isaac. He split the wood
for the burnt offering, and he set out for the place of which
God had told him. On the third day Abraham looked up and
saw the place from afar. Then Abraham said to his servants,
"You stay here with the ass. The boy and I will go up there;
we will worship, and we will return to you." Abraham took
the wood for the burnt offering and put it on his son Isaac. He
himself took the firestone and the knife, and the two walked
off together. Then Isaac said to his father Abraham, "Father!"
And he answered, "Yes, my son." And he said, "Here are the
firestone and the wood, but where is the sheep for the burnt
offering?" And Abraham said, "It is God who will see to the
sheep for this burnt offering, my son." And the two of them
walked on together. They arrived at the place of which God
had told him. Abraham built an altar there; he laid out the
wood; he bound his son Isaac; he laid him on the altar, on
top of the wood. And Abraham picked up the knife to slay his
son. Then a messenger of יהוה called to him from heaven:
"Abraham! Abraham!" And he answered, "Here I am."

II

I am   your favored one   whom you love

                                                              I will

      split the wood

            the place   You stay

                        my

                        burnt

                                          altar

                                    called

                                                    "Here I am."

III

                  I am

split.

                                                    I will go

      to

            the wood

                  the place

                                          I am.

23

Ram in the Thicket

Everything bends. But the sunlight
fractured to stained glass
by branches—tamarisk, carob—
cups me, a green cathedral, a green

grief. Curtain of boughs drawn
behind me. Though I've been dispatched
as an offering, I tarry. The leaves
are sweet and I don't want my time

to end with a blade any more
than Isaac does. Soon we will all be
story, the mountain vanished
in a blinking edge.

Abraham and Isaac will not speak
again.

Landscape with Animated Deer

Now winter, thorny boughs, the cold
to stand against, everything
visible as breath, near-breaking.
And this herd, their bodies spooled
wire and lights. The rigid *bow,*
lift, bow of their heads just hammers home
how useless grazing is to them
in their empty frames. Even so,
their faces seem familiar and kind,
and I see myself in the tight
wire armature, studded with lights
that blink and flicker into wind.
They shed their pale glow over the lawn,
casting themselves against the house
and shrubs with a selfless animal grace,
as when, in a predawn blur years gone,
I walked the spine of a hill in the thaw
of another winter's death, and saw
a deer step to the edge of the wood.
I was lit by that flare, the electric blood.

Abraham

God will ask the same
of you. You name your son
held by the heel and he dreams
of beating God on the mat. He names
his son *one who adds*, another
dreamer of sheaves. We accrue
our sacrifices, and the world
is warmed by need until
the mountains begin melting.
What will you offer now
in the woven nest
that will hatch instead of bleed?

Sarah

Avarice was my snake. My name
for you was a testament
to my own surprise. I sent your half-
brother into the desert
like sowing half the land with lye,
like sucking salty
olives as the groves burned.

In the Beginning (בְּרֵאשִׁית)

This was the year of no touch
but the touch of our own hands,
our breath pressed to our own
faces. In the beginning

anything could kill us,
and then we learned it was the breath
in our exhalation
that would kill us. The trees'

green leaves and the garbage
bags taped at the nurses' wrists.
Particulate invisible
death, from which we hid

in our rooms that were empty
of time. The screens that turned us
into portraits
for one another—*Here I am.*

When a baby is birthed we say she is crowning,
cupped in the breath of the world.

Exhibit S: *Añoranza*

We lit a candle, and the flame spread until the sky was singed with it. The fire shed scales and petals and eyes. We dipped our fingers into the whirlpools of the shadows. We were skullcapped. We were cut eyeholes in the cloth to see. We put our arms around one another, and this framed a circle with four chambers. Two aortas, two ventricles, four tunnels to the past. One of us missing the lips to speak. One of us blindfolded. And at the center—a baby, her roseate hand extended. The ripple of candlelight like muscle across my inside.

Mount Moriah

Dust and rocks and sunlight a slap
in the face. The knuckle bones
of tree roots gripping the earth.
I've been calling through the altitude
for years, find God's
profile in the overlook.
My body doesn't want to climb.

In Order

Abraham, his shadow before him on the mountain pass. Behind him bends Isaac, the unknowing future. Cast a shadow or cast lots. Doubt, cast out. Enough, as in, you have suffered enough. Father Abraham. Gematria transforms numbers into letters, as does the sonnet. Hebrew on my tongue, the aftertaste of chocolate. In Hebrew, the Bible is written in future perfect. Just an endlessly mutable future that makes up our past. Kike, what no one has called me, yet. Lest we forget. Mind, as in I will not. Not now. Or will I bend as the reeds bend to wind. Perfect, as in, flawless. Question: Where do I go when I've lost my roots? Roots, as in, what feeds the tree. Silver losses, accretion of mercury in the saddle of a dream. Tomorrow. Until nothing is left. Vacancy. Will sacrifice, not would sacrifice, not wood. X is an eye crossed out. You will, I will, he will, they will. Zealot is another word for believing without question.

Swing, Age 10

You strain against the other swingers'
   contrapuntal threads
      of creaking, watch a girl
   try to pull herself neck
to neck with you, but you don't hold
         her hand and your arcs ramp apart.
           You watch boys jump from their flung seats,
launch themselves, bombs
      without fuses to light them.
          The trouble with swings is, no matter how
      hard
         you kick your legs, everyone's body
    is soaring the same
       as yours. You think, they cannot know
what suffering is. The bulb
of your mind refuses
to flower. You pump harder.

Years from Then

I am sitting on the lawn in front of my house with two high school classmates. We are studying math. We are taking a break, drinking lemonade. Airily, full of light, one of them mentions a crime in this neighborhood. It is my father's crime. The headline: "Newton Man Stabs Mother-in-Law." It was on this lawn that she ran from him. It was on this lawn that she bled from the wounds he cut into her. I wasn't there to see it happen. Instead, I picture it in my mind, as I always do: I'm in the sunlight, surrounded by cops. The driveway is painted red and blue in couplets. There is yellow tape everywhere, like a highlighter highlighting the most important absences. The neighbors are not talking, just like I am not talking with my classmates—about an absence, a hole in the cosmos, an anti-name. Do you see crime inscribed on my face with its blank (blanked-out) look? Shall we return to the sine and cosine, to curves and the spaces under them? The answers are in the back of the book but only for the even-numbered problems. The odd are up to us.

O

O is the circle in which we sit before my mother opens her mouth to speak. The sun shines summer, and the lawn of the house where we are staying is a flat field. We are here to escape the policemen searching our house, the thing my mother is about to tell us after this breath. We are a seven-sitting circle: adults and children and a baby. When this pause ends, there will be words like the smell of meat frying. My mother cannot help but be the pause, the mouthful of air before the vacuum that pulls knowledge into our ears. The pause is a flat field—nothing is meant to grow there, but it does. The pause cannot help but be the thing that comes before the thing that ends the world. It cannot help.

The many rabbis are like many suns / in the same sky, too much glow
for one page of Talmud, / eager examples—how to
honor both their fathers and their / mothers. Honoring your mother is the same
as honoring God: "as if I had sat / among them" is the exact
quote. Rabbi A's "demented" dad / asked for water then fell   asleep and A
bent above his nodding head, / waiting, cup in hand. Rabbi T lay   his
hands on the ground so his mother's feet / would not touch dirt. Are these to be
my exemplars? When love gets / tough, what then? Rabbi A (not the same A)
watched his mother "go crazy," left / for Israel to pray for her, then learned
she was following him. Calling / the public gaze toward my parent's
madness—is this honor? / As ever, two opinions in the Talmud: one says
if she's cared for, he can leave her, / one says he should have never left her.

Rabbis argue across centuries: no echo sounds back to them, nor back to me.

Honor thy father and thy mother   ## Thou shalt revere thy mother and father

"Honoring one's father and one's mother are of equal importance"—the Rambam, but

if they both want a drink of water / what is a child to do? She must serve her
father. Here, water, even if you sleep / in the pit of despair, I will wait for you, Father.
I pour a jug of water for him, / pouring cracked streams while his back is turned and
do you see anywhere / my mother in this? She does not

belong in these poems, Rabbi.

"Happy is one who never saw his parents" Rabbi Y (not the same Y) wrote,
since it's impossible / to honor them enough. Not just
holding a pitcher to cracked lips, / holding your tongue if your mother
tosses money into the sea. / I honor you, Ima, by leaving you outside
these poems; you, Abba, / by holding you inside them.

Who Spreads the Land Upon the Water
(רוֹקַע הָאָרֶץ עַל הַמָּיִם)

Let me tell you about God's and
my argument about sand—

how come it works so hard to disperse?
I'm talking about the sand

in your shoes, in your pant cuffs,
you shake out your towel but there's sand

in the car when you get home and then
what good is that? It's not like some sand-

y beaches are going to spring up
in my car, in my backyard, like sand

will pollinate and flower into
tropical beaches of soft pink sand,

the sift and grit of it won't
colonize the planet. So what's sand's

point then? And God said
sand isn't sentient, sand

doesn't try to spread like that, if you'd just
stay off the beach then the sand

would stay put. The places you've been
are changed by you. I grind sand

from rocks, God said, don't you
believe I could keep the sand

in one place if I needed to? I don't
know what you need, God. Understand-

ing isn't something that comes easy
to me. At night I worry the sand

from under my nails, I heat milk
for cocoa and then the sand

in my teeth turns it gritty.
I'm trying to say, the sand

is glory, sugar, and glare. The sand
kisses gritrock, licks formations

slick as footprints in the sand.
God, I've seen your sky divided.

Calves, Drumlin Farm

From the fenced edge, I watch them
stir the bare shoulders
of pasture. I want to be
with them, want to stand
in the warm press of many.
For the first time, these calves
must bow their heads
to feed, their lips loosening grass,
not the urge of their mothers'
bodies. There was a time I knew
how to draw love from my mother,
how to relieve the pressure
under her skin by taking.

Name

We were having a read-a-thon at school, and I asked him what name he wanted me to write down on the read-a-thon form—Aharon or Aaron. Hebrew or English on the official line of my money-making form. I always called him Abba, which means father. And the grown-ups called him "Ron" or "Ronnie." Aharon or Aaron both held Ron inside of themselves. Did he want to exist in Hebrew or English? And when I asked him this, his face contorted into something I didn't recognize—not anger but hate. He said, "You don't know my name?" I saw in his face my loss of him. I fled that room to spare us the loss. His names intact. He doesn't choose between his American self and his self that sleeps in Hebrew under the ground, like the ruins I've never seen in Jerusalem, a whole city under a city, a whole name under a name. Let him be Abba—the sun in the sky but cold, shining with hard white light that will not change.

Exhibit S: *¿Arrepentida?*

Portrait of a mother and her
leaf-sleep, her lamb flame,
her infant sheep with its gold
crown now turning to stone.

Underneath her skin
is the universe, dizzy with stars, lit
on fire. Justice,
take off my skin, and underneath
the softest flesh-fur.
The hand on the brow.

Slips of the Tongue

Not delusion but deluge
Not deluded but diluted

Not psychosis but psyche
Not antipsychotic but antidote

Not a state hospital but a prison
Not a prescription but a sentence

Not the magnolia petals raining down in spirals outside my window
I do not know what your favorite tree is, I will never

Not what frightens you—the microwave, people
On the beach—not even God

That metallic taste is
Not blood but a key on my tongue

That water like diving into the ocean
Through the open mouth of a cave

Do you remember the natural bridge
You promised to take me when I got older

Now I am older with no one to tell me
If the bridge has eroded, if you—

Exhibit X: Inadmissable

Exhibit P is closed until further notice due to the pandemic. Exhibit N is off limits to the public; inside it, I am waiting for someone to find me. The opening of Exhibit M has been delayed to make room for what is missing. The funding for Exhibit R has been cut. Exhibit T will go unopened. Exhibit Y is the palpable distance of the body wearing the body, the sweat sheen halo, the agitation of the fixer tray in the darkroom, the inner distance, where have you gone to? Here I am.

Minor God

This crab could be the oracle: see how his eye stalks are portents, and in his ancient mouth the mandibles click like clock gears. He holds time in his mouth. And it opens, as if to pour tenderly the contents of the future onto the sand that is dark with rain. The shine of his shell is a looking pool where the sky can see its face. This crab with its leg jousts, claw joints, and articulations, knows something about being broken open. Knows that escape happens sideways, scuttling under rocks where everything else is starfish and seaweed and barnacle blasted to stone and trying to hold on.

Like Love Angry Surprised

faces faces maps
like feathers like sand
tendrils winding between the news
and joy
like gold like sweat
what you have feasted on or wish to
if your longing
runs parallel to my own
like fact like love
scrolling through you

Sharon Olds Goes Back to May 1937

She doesn't mention how on the horizon
the Hindenberg is going down in flames
that same month and year. It's the end
of the airship era. It's the end of giant
metal whales glinting in the sky,
the end of their balloon bodies resisting
weather. Maybe the blood in the tiles
behind her father's head is also flames.
I know these get confused for me sometimes,
Sharon. Like a dragon, fire
floods out of the nose
of the Hindenberg in a pilgrim's diode.
Like a dragon, sparks spark into children.

Exhibit S: Belkis Ayón

I come to the exhibit masked. 2020, we are each a walking viral load. Still, I have to see. Aunque no te conozco, Belkis, I know you. The dreams that won't let go. The pressure sea exerts on island. Your llanto reaches across oceans, as far as the land of the dead. You gave its figures bodies. You gave us the texture of a circle by tracing the negative eggs, the holes in the cluster. The math of scales. Blanco y negro y gris, you coated the collagraphy, you set metal plates in their tectonics. You haunted the rooms. Dame la mano, the one with the paint and the palm. The one with the wheat and the flame.

Exhibit S: *Pa' que me quieras por siempre*

Leaves on fire, something to hold the loss. The only jar deep enough is the flower at the base of the skull. A flame blossoming in my hand and a knife in the opposite palm. The darkness kneeling with its hands full of wheat. Knee deep in the threshing, oh stand back. Wheat is feathers, wheat is the delicate plates of the skull fusing, refusing. Belkis, cross my back with plated armor, my knuckles with scales. Let my palms be the ones puckering with fish.

Star Colossus

I was born a giant. I held fire
in one hand, the book of justice
in the other. I was born to metal
and flame, the rain and sea
cooled me, I greened as a forest.
It is not enough
to pull into my harbor—
now I stand at a locked door
without gold. The waters rise
and rise and my torch can't
burn underwater. Instead
each joint and joist of me
will rise in a constellation.
I will burn among the stars,
visible from any ocean.

Laurel

Tonight the light turns
its back, the gold blues and blackens
the trees' reaching arms

that hold, as dancers do,
the ringed emptiness
before them, like women

holding out to their children
their longing. He turned
her into a tree for running

from another he. Shiver
of sunlight in the boughs.

Who Revives the Dead (מְחַיֶּה הַמֵּתִים)

None of us imagined ourselves here,
but here we are. The storefronts are all burnt,
the school, the synagogue, the graves all burnt.
Wind and ashes harrowing the air.
We set sail, knowing we would not return
to our homeland, the bricks and windows burnt
dull black, the books, trunks, cinder blocks all burnt
behind us. Even memories are burnt,

some burned to death, some burned on altars
in the public square, the sites chosen
by history. If there exists in heaven
anyone like a god,
let him know hard fire, a thicket
of pain on pain. Then we will know he's present.

Exhibit S: *La Cena*

Profile with one eye open, blindfold
like gauze stuffed into a wound
backwards. The fish uneaten,
as if this could undo the supper's
ending, its lastness.

Don't let me see
the fish bones branch
the dark air shiver
the white dish piled with red and silver.
Oh hide my eye
in the mountains, between
my fingers, cast down
my gaze.

Moshiach in Mariupol

Every repetition of collapse—sheets of Sheetrock, car
carcasses, paint flakes in the amber air—and bodies,

crumpled, explicit, ordinary, no breath in them. A hand
waving as the train pulls west. But see him there,

slumped in the rubble, sifting ash into piles, waiting
for someone to finally recognize him so he can reveal

the gold in the grain. The blood that waters
trees. The nuclear thrum. The bodies

stand up, brush off the dust, the roof tiles
return to the roofs like a flock of pigeons.

The bomb smoke gathers itself in handfuls,
or in a pillar, how a host lead us. After

all the loss, we find ourselves stunned
in the open mouths of houses, we hear

the sorrow angels hear when God's throat opens
and the Word comes out.

How to Write a Poem
After Abraham

Arc of stars
along your leap:
what will move
through you.
Ram's horn curled round
the moon and its shadow.
The sky debrided.
Here—the needle
and the suture thread
and the steady hand
and the eye.

Exhibit S: *Ya estamos aquí*

The dark familial
The snake-draped lap
The startled pupil
The limp penis
The bowl of fish
The hieroglyph
The candle turns into a lily
The hills tesseract
The most frightened one
Takes down the crucifix
Will the goat nuzzle under
The priest's cloak
Will the sky be cold
Will death have palms
Will the grass ignite
Will the antimatter
Oh spotted one will you
Lift the curtain
Show your face

The Mirror in His Pocket

God came to me in the early hours. Not in a cloud or a pillar of light but a sudden gust, ghost, or hologram. God put on my makeup: rose-gold eyeshadow, pinch-me blush, concealer like rain falling into an arroyo. Memory of my fifth-grade dance, arms around a boy's flushed neck as we swayed to "Stairway to Heaven." God braided strands of gold into my nightgown. Every time I tossed and turned, I shimmered. God watered the twin trunks of my legs, the green blades of my feet. *There*, God said. He drew a compact mirror from His pocket. I was too illuminated to have a reflection. Then He put a piece of the moon in my hand. It weighed five hundred tons. It was so dense it pulled all of the room, the sunlight slanting in like a rhyme, the sleeping twenty-month-old next door, the automatic sprinklers and the shuttered headstones, into its heart. *Why did you give me this, God?* God clicked the mirror shut.

Notes

Epigraphs:

Hebrew text of Genesis with English translation was accessed via Sefaria.com

The body:

Two of the poems have titles that are accompanied by Hebrew words in parentheses. "In the Beginning," is accompanied by בְּרֵאשִׁית, Bereshit, the Hebrew word for Genesis which literally means "in the beginning" or "at first." "The Eating Knife" is accompanied by הַמַּאֲכֶלֶת, Ha'Ma'achelet, which is the Hebrew word in the Bible for Abraham's knife. Ma'achelet's word root is "ochel" or food, suggesting the knife was a knife used for eating or food.

Four of the poems take their titles and subject matter (indirectly) from blessings that are recited on a daily basis, at different key points throughout the day. The four blessings cited in these poems are a small fraction of the total blessings that can be recited in a given day. Each of the poems beginning with "who" is titled after a prayer suffix. Each prayer begins, "Blessed are you Lord our God, king of the universe, who—" and then an attribute of God that helps express gratitude, hope, and/or pleading. The specific prayers being cited are as follows:

שֶׁעָשַׂנִי בְּצַלְמוֹ (She'asani Betzelmo) is the blessing suffix "who made me in your image," thanking God for making humans "in His image" per the story of Adam and Eve. This prayer is recited as part of the set of blessings in the Shacharit or morning prayer.

רוֹקַע הָאָרֶץ עַל הַמָּיִם (Rokah Ha'aretz Al Hamayim) is the blessing suffix "who spreads the land above the water." It is part of the set of blessings in the Shacharit or morning prayer.

מְחַיֶּה הַמֵּתִים (Mehayeh Ha'meytim) is the blessing suffix of the prayer we say to bless God's power to give life or maintain life. Death is the other side of this equation. The phrase literally means, "who enlivens the dead" or "who breaths life into the dead."

Five of the poems are ekphrastic poems based on prints by the Cuban artist Belkis Ayón. Each ekphrastic poem is titled after the print that it is based on, following the prefix "Exhibit S." For example, "Exhibit S: *Añoranza*" is a poem written after Belkis Ayon's print, *Añoranza (Yearning)*. The list of titles with translations is:

Añoranza (Yearning)
Ya estamos aquí (We are already here)
Pa' que me quieras por siempre (So you will want me forever)
La cena (The supper)
¿Arrepentida? (Repentant?)

I viewed these works of Ayón at the retrospective exhibit *Nkame* that was hosted by the University of Oregon's Jordan Schnitzer Museum of Art in 2021. Thanks to John Weber, director of the museum, for giving me permission to view the collection. Thanks to the Belkis Ayón Estate for their generous permission allowing me to use Ayón's titles as my own in tribute of her work and life. May her memory be for a blessing, *Zichronah Livrachah* (z"l).

"Sharon Olds Goes Back to May 1937" references Sharon Olds' poem "I Go Back to May 1937."

In the poem "Who Made Me In Your Image," the mechitzah is the divider or curtain separating men from women during prayers. There is a mechitzah at the Kotel Ha'ma'aravi or Western Wall in Jerusalem.

In the poem "Moshiach in Mariupol," the Moshiach refers to the Jewish messiah, who has not yet come.

Acknowledgments

Thanks to the editors of the journals in which versions of these poems first appear, sometimes with different titles or in different versions:

Bellingham Review: "Self-Portrait as Isaac"
Boats Against the Current: "Stenotype"
CLOVES Literary: "Years from Then"
Cream City Review: "O"
FED: "Exhibit S: *Ya Estamos Aqui*," "Exhibit S: *La Cena*"
Gulf Coast: "MMMBop Was Released"
Indianapolis Review: "Exhibit S: Añoranza"
Jewish Literary Journal: "Abraham"
Michigan Quarterly Review: "How to Write a Poem After
 Abraham"
Pleiades: "Element"
Pendemics Journal: "Calves, Drumlin Farm"
Tupelo Quarterly: "Altar," "The Voice of God," "Minor
 God," "In the Beginning," "The Eating Knife"
Whale Road Review: "Laurel"

"Landscape with Animated Deer" appeared in the anthology *Turn*, with thanks to editor Laura LeHew. "Star Colossus" appears on the website of the American Jewish Historical Society.

Thanks to the Joiner Center Writer's Workshop, the Yiddish Book Center for a TENT fellowship, and the Martha's Vineyard Institute for Creative Writing for a parent-writer fellowship.

Thanks to my teachers: Tom DePeter z"l, Barbara Helfgott Hyett and Eric Hyett of PoemWorks, Rick Benjamin, Forrest Gander, C.D. Wright z"l, Catherine Imbriglio, Linda Gregerson, Lorna Goodison, Anne Carson, Thylias Moss, Richard Tillinghast, Khaled Mattawa, Keith Taylor, Lisa Olstein, Sabrina Orah Mark, Annie Rogers, and Sandra Beasley.

Thanks to my friends who are poets and novelists, thinkers and feelers, whose own work, compassionate and attentive reading, and creative thinking nurtured and inspired the images and thoughts that led to these poems. Special thanks to Celeste Ng for being amazing and to Rabbi Ruhi Sophia Motzkin Rubenstein for the invitation to engage with Genesis 22.

Thanks to Rita Mookerjee for the title, Taylor Byas for the brilliant editing, Derek Mong for the last-minute edits, and Rosebud Ben-Oni for the important questions.

Thanks to my family for their support of the work, even when it's difficult to read. Special thanks to Maddie, for the ways she embodies my connection to art and love.

Thank you to my therapists for helping me heal.

Thanks to my husband, Jon Krier, and to each of my children: *You are my very favorite thing.*

Biography

Ayelet Amittay is a poet and psychiatric nurse practitioner in Eugene, Oregon. Her poems appear or are forthcoming in *Gulf Coast*, *Rattle*, *Michigan Quarterly Review*, *Tupelo Quarterly*, and others. She has received fellowships from the Yiddish Book Center and the Martha's Vineyard Institute of Creative Writing. She can be found at ayeletpoet.com or on social media @ayeletpoet.

Title Index

First Line Index